Wilbur Wison Thoburn

The Life and Teachings of Christ

A Study of Christian Ideals and Their Application to Life

Wilbur Wison Thoburn

The Life and Teachings of Christ
A Study of Christian Ideals and Their Application to Life

ISBN/EAN: 9783337027551

Printed in Europe, USA, Canada, Australia, Japan

Cover: Foto ©Lupo / pixelio.de

More available books at **www.hansebooks.com**

THE LIFE AND TEACHINGS OF CHRIST

A

STUDY OF CHRISTIAN IDEALS AND THEIR APPLICATION TO LIFE

SYLLABUS OF A COURSE OF
LECTURES DELIVERED IN LELAND STANFORD JUNIOR UNIVERSITY

—BY—

WILBUR W. THOBURN

UNIVERSITY PRESS
STANFORD UNIVERSITY, CALIFORNIA
1896

LECTURE I.

INTRODUCTION.

I. Why do we study Christ and Christianity?
  1. Because Christianity alone sustains a steadily advancing civilization.
  2. Because Christianity marks the highest point reached in the development of man's moral and religious nature.
     a. It differs from all other religions in obeying the law of development.
  3. Because the breadth and universality of Christianity are derived solely from the faith and inspiration of its founder.
  4. Because Christ alone tells who and what man is.
     a. Individualism.
     b. Altruism.
  5. Because Christ alone tells who God is.
     a. All other definitions have been overtaken by man in his development.
     b. Father. Liberty and dependence.

II. Conditions of study.
  1. Willingness to follow the truth.
  2. Prejudice. Open-mindedness.

III. Methods of study.
  1. Unscientific.
     a. Divides all religions into true and false.
     b. Regards the true religion as from God and all others from men.
     c. Regards the true as inspired, the others as invented.
  Note.—This method inconsistent with any scientific study.
  2. Scientific.
     a. Regards the highest as the outgrowth of all the lower.
     b. Comparison.
     c. Studies the actual as well as the ideal.
  3. Scientific method gains in material.
     a. Does it risk vitality?
  Note.—The full content of any religious system can not be measured by any intellectual process.

IV. Sources of information.
  1. History.
     a. Profane and sacred.
        [1] Should this distinction be made?
     b. Modern social and political institutions.
     c. The subjective element. (Hyde, Social Theology, 68-69.)
     d. Impossible to study the historical Christ alone. (Martineau, A Study of Religion, I, 1. Strausse, Life of Jesus, I, x.)

LECTURE II.

EVOLUTION OF RELIGION.

I. Difficulties of discussion.
  1. Misconceptions concerning religion.
  2. Fear of heterodoxy.
      a. Was not Jesus a heretic?
  3. Conservatism of theology.
  4. Relation between man's conception of God and his intelligence.
      a. Religion a synthesis of reason and faith.
  5. Is the religious life an exception to the laws of life?
  6. Are we to start with an assumption of perfection for Christianity, or shall we approach it from the race side? (Drummond, Ascent of Man, 112.)
  7. Survivals — vestigial organs.

II. Opposing views of man.
  1. Struggling to regain a state of former excellence now lost.
  2. Struggling to reach perfection, never known hence never lost.
  3. Difference between innocence and virtue.
  4. The doctrine of "the fall."

III. The course of the evolution of religion.
  1. Like all history its beginnings are lost.
      a. Aid from psychology.
      b. Lessons from childhood.
      c. Conjecture from what man has put behind him.
  2. Naturism. Indistinct, chaotic. (Fiske, Idea of God, 63-64. Ency. Brit., art. Religion.)
      a. Animism—personification of the forces of nature. Echo, shadow.
      b. Fear made the first gods.
      c. A god is the projection into infinity of a human ideal.
      d. The idea of the devil in primitive religions. Inversely as the conception of one Supreme Being.
  3. Polydæmonistic religions.
  4. Therianthropic polytheism.
  5. Anthropomorphic polytheism.
  6. Increasing definitiveness of idea of the soul.
  7. Ethical element. Its appearance and development.

IV. Ethical religions.
  1. National.
      a. Confucianism.
      b. Brahminism.
      c. Judaism.
  2. Semi-universal.
      a. Islamism. Exalts God and degrades man.
      b. Buddhism. Exalts man and ignores God.
  4. Requirements of a universal religion.
      a. It must be spiritual.
      b. It must recognize man's freedom.
      c. It must recognize equality and brotherhood of man.
      d. It must recognize the unity and fatherhood of God.
  5. Does Christianity meet these requirements? This is the question we ask of Jesus.

LECTURE III.

THE HISTORICAL BASIS.

I. Division into sacred and profane history.
   1. Should this separation be made?
       a. Why should the Bible stand apart from other records? (See Lecture IV.)

II. The historical basis two-fold.
   1. The fact. The life of Jesus.
   2. The historical development.

III. Division of subject, considering all records.
   1. The testimony of secular history as to the origin and early progress of Christianity, including personal character, spirit, and aims of early Christians.
   2. The authority and contents of the early records of Christianity. The New Testament.
   3. The effect of Christianity on the intellectual, moral, and social life of the world.
   Note. — A fourth line of study might be added — namely, the foreshadowings of Old Testament history. This is not considered in this discussion.

IV. Secular history.
   1. No facts, not recorded in Scripture, are furnished by contemporary history.
       a. Tacitus, 55–117 A. D.
       b. Suetonius, 72–140 A. D.
       c. Pliny the younger.
       d. Josephus.
           [1] Character and history. Christian interpolations.
           [2] Antiquities. XVIII, v, 2; XX, ix, 1; XVIII, iii, 3.
       e. Talmud. (See art. Jesus, Ency. Brit., 659.)

LECTURE IV.

THE BIBLICAL BASIS.

I. Relation of Bible to Christ.

II. Why is the Bible called a Holy Book ?
 1. Compare with other sacred books of the world.
 2. The question of inspiration from a scientific view.
 3. Is its position in the world due to dogma or inherent power?
    a. The test of spiritual truthfulness is spiritual fruitfulness.

III. Revelation.
 1. Is it from without or within?
    a. The unfolding of the divine in human consciousness.
    b. Were the ten commandments true before Moses wrote them ?
 2. Revelation progressive.

IV. Relation of Bible to theology.
 1. Infallibility and inerrancy.
 2. Chiefly a book of religion.
 3. Its symbolism the stumbling block of theology and the help of religion.

V. The Bible defined and described.
 1. Various canons.
 2. Higher criticism.
 3. Its place in literature of the world.

VI. The New Testament.
 1. The question of authorship.
 2. The purpose of the writers. (Cambridge Bible, introduction, pp. 14–17.)
 3. The history comparatively meager.
 4. Probable order of growth.
    a. Oral teaching.
    b. Memorizing.
    c. Gradual commission to writing.
    d. Editing of these fragments by some authority.

i

LECTURE V.

THE LAND AND THE PEOPLE.

I. Palestine.
    1. Location: relation to Egypt; to the East; to Rome.
    2. The cross-road of commerce.
    3. Mixture of highland and valley.
    4. Its natural defences: mountain and desert.
    5. Its water systems. Its coast lines.
    6. The climate; its extreme variation.
    7. Relation of topography and climate to the character of the people; to their literature; to their religion. (Farrar, Life of Christ, 5.)

II. The people.

III. The political condition of the world at the time of Christ.
    1. United under one scepter.
    2. Internal peace; freedom of trade; commercial security.
    3. Educational value of commerce.
    4. Relation of peace and commercial security to morals.
    5. Augustus: centralization. (Gibbon, III., 120.)
    6. Relation between political conditions and theological conceptions.

IV. Social and moral conditions.
    1. Religions of antiquity worn out. (Farrar, Life of Christ, 25.)
    2. "The Syrian Orontes had flowed into the Tiber." (Juv. Sat., III, 69.)
    3. Morality divorced from religion.
    4. Relations between these conditions and the coming of Christ. Compare Luther's Reformation, and French Revolution.

V. The Jewish world at the time of Christ.
    1. The Roman conquest.
    2. Herod. The division of the kingdom, 4 B. C.
        a. Cæsarea Philippi. Philip.
        b. Galilee and Peræa. Herod Antipas.
        c. Idumæa, Judæa. Samaritis, Archelaus.
        d. Deposed 6 A. D. Procurators.
    3. The Sanhedrim. Its composition; its jurisdiction; the priests; the sects.

VI. The expectation of the Messiah.
1. Its growth. Encouraged by the rabbis. Read into the sacred writings. Increased with the desolation of Israel. Influence on literature, education, and politics.

VII. The Jewish conception of the Messiah.
1. A great prince. A conqueror. A world-wide kingdom. A paradise for the Jew. (Geikie, Life of Christ, I, 77.)
2. The Messianic idea independent of Jesus.

LECTURES VI-VII.

THE BIRTH OF JESUS.

I. Biography always written backward.
   The law of myth: increases with the square of distance. Were the Gospels independent of this law? Shall we criticise the Gospels as we would any other biography?

II. Facts to be granted.
   1. The Gospels were really written * by their reputed authors.
   2. Each wrote believing that the events he narrated actually occurred.
   3. Each production has been subjected to the severest criticism.
   4. Many have denied, no one has thus far offered, a natural explanation for the unnatural events.

III. Two points of view: religion; science.
   Shall we believe all things until they are shown to be false, or, believe nothing until it is shown to be true?

IV. Intellect and faith.
   Spencer, Principles of Sociology:
      The emotions influence conduct more than reason, p. 308.
      Utilitarian belief inadequate, p. 308, c.
      Intellect imperfect guide, p. 308, a.
      Actions determined chiefly by feeling, p. 307, b.
      Mystery, p. 310, c.

V. Materialism. Defined: contrast with spiritualism.

VI. Natural and supernatural.
   1. Folly of dual conception.
   2. The natural that part of truth which we know or think we know. The supernatural yet to be known.
   3. The mysteries of today ever becoming the realities of tomorrow.
   4. Will the miracles be explained? (Farrar, Life of Christ, preface, ix-xi. Strausse, Life of Christ, I, 195.)
   5. Relation to Christ's teaching.

* See Lecture IV — vi, d.

VII. Different positions toward the miracles.
1. Accept them literally, as violations of natural law; necessary to Christ's mission.
2. Explain them, if possible, by natural laws.
3. Reject them as unnatural, and with them Christianity.
4. Believe them and wait for the explanation, which, if it ever comes, will not be a violation of law.

Read Luke, i, 80.

VIII. The story of miraculous birth in Gospel history.
1. Mentioned only by Matthew and Luke.
2. Never referred to by Christ or by any of the Apostolic epistles.
3. Contrast with the story of the resurrection.
4. The position of the skeptic contrasted with the believer in the supernatural.
5. Agnosticism and the search after truth.

IX. The lineage of Jesus. (Matt., i, 1-17. Luke, iii, 23-38.)
1. Matthew's object to show Jesus as the national hero, the successor of Abraham and David.
2. Luke's object to exhibit Christ as the founder of universal religion.
3. Contrast the two. (Camb. Bib., Lk., Excursus II, 369.)

X. The forerunner. (Lk., i, 5-25; 57-66. See Lecture IX.)
1. Relation of the Baptist to Christ.
2. To the Jewish conception of Elijah and the Messiah.

XI. The birth of Jesus.
1. Date and circumstances.
2. Joseph and Mary.
3. Dreams and visions.
4. The census.
5. Bethlehem; its inn.

XII. The Magi.
1. The star. Alford's theory.

XIII. The shepherds.
1. The evidence of the manger. The sign of the Messiah was his lowliness.

XIV. The flight into Egypt. (Matthew, ii, 13-21.) Herod.

XV. Return to Nazareth.

LECTURE VIII.

THE BOYHOOD OF JESUS.

I. Nazareth. Location, surroundings, history, reputation.
II. The choice of a home.
    1. The fear of Archelaus. Its significance.
    2. Influence of Nazareth on character of Jesus.
    3. The carpenter.
III. The "Son of Man."
    1. Are there indications of a remarkable childhood? The child with the halo.
    2. The unfolding character.
    3. Like other children.
    4. Meager details of his childhood. (Beecher, Life of Christ, I, 75.)
IV. The Jewish boy.
    1. Education.
    2. Trade.
V. Evidence of education.
    1. Never attended the schools of the rabbis. (Mark vi, 2; John vi, 42.)
    2. He had learned to write. (John viii, 6.)
    3. Acquainted with Aramaic, Hebrew, Greek, and Latin. (Farrar, Life of Christ, I, 91.)
    4. Impressed by nature.
VI. The boy in the temple.
    1. The occasion — Passover.
    2. The dispute with the doctors.
    3. The mother's question.
VII. His father's business.
    1. Was Jesus conscious of his greatness?
    2. The ministry of youth unwholesome.
    3. His life a revelation to himself.
    4. He was subject to his parents.

Contemporaneous History.

B. C. 3. — Octavianus Augustus had been sole ruler of the Roman Empire from B. C. 30. Twice during that period the temple of Janus had been closed in sign of peace.

B. C. 1. — Death of Herod. Rising of the Jews against the Procurator Sabinus. Repression of the revolt by Varus; two thousand Jews crucified.

A. D. 6. — Resistance to the Census of Quirinus by Judas the Gaulonite and his Galilean followers.

A. D. 7. — Banishment of Archelaus.

A. D. 1–12. — Campaigns against the Germans, Pannonians, and Dalmatians, conducted by Tiberius and Germanicus. The disastrous defeats of Varus in Germany. Final success and triumph of the Roman generals.

A. D. 14. — Death of Augustus and succession of Tiberius.

A. D. 15–17. — Germanicus continues the war against the Germans and triumphs.

A. D. 18. — Death of Ovid and Livy.

A. D. 1 . — Death of Germanicus. Jews banished from Italy.

A. D. 20–31. — Hateful tyranny of Tiberius. Ascendancy of Sejanus. Fall of Sejanus, A. D. 30.

A. D. 26. — Pontius Pilate appointed as the sixth Procurator of Judæa.

LECTURE IX.

THE VOICE IN THE WILDERNESS.

I. John the Baptist.
   1. Relation to Christ.
   2. Expectation concerning Elijah.
   3. The historical crisis.
   4. His character. Burdened with a great sorrow and a great ideal.
   5. His appearance. Customs and habits of the Nazarites.
   6. Scene of his teaching.
   7. His audience.

II. John's message.
   1. A warning and a proclamation.
   2. Repentance.
   3. The "phrases" of religion.
   4. The Kingdom of Heaven; meanings of the term in the New Testament.
   5. Morality *versus* legalism.

III. Baptism.
   1. Among the Jews.
   2. John's use and meaning.
   3. The added meaning of Christ.
   4. The use and abuse of forms.

IV. The doctrines of the Baptist.
   1. John's conception of Christ.
   2. Christ's conception of John.
   3. "The least in the Kingdom greater than he."

V. Asceticism.
   1. May spring from:
      a. Arrogance.
      b. Satiety.
      c. Selfish fear.
      d. Consciousness of a mission.
   2. When asceticism becomes a crime.

VI. The baptism of Jesus.
  1. Incident.
  2. Insight of John.
  3. The significance of the act.
     a. Self-recognition.
     b. Public declaration.
     c. Rupture with the temple.
  4. The vision.

VII. John in prison.
  1. Antipas and the Baptist.
  2. John's questioning disciples.
  3. His death.

LECTURE X.

THE TEMPTATIONS.

(Matt. iv, 1-11 : Mk. i, 12-13 ; Lk. iv, 1-13.)

I. The circumstance.
 1. A bit of personal history.
 2. Cause of trial.

II. The tempter.
 1. The devils of religion.
 2. Christ's adversary.
 3. The Jewish conception of the wilderness.

III. Could Jesus sin ? (Heb. v, 8.)
 1. The position of theology.
 2. The need of the heart.

IV. The forty days.
 1. Fasting in the East.
 2. Weighing the consequences.
 3. Casting the die.

V. The first trial.
 1. Expressed figuratively.
 2. The struggle for bread and comfort.
 3. Mahomet's answer.
 4. Modern examples.
  a. Bread and butter values.
  b. The battle in society ; in the church.
 5. Christ's answer.

VI. The second trial.
 1. Appeal to wonder and imagination.
 2. Has the church surrendered ?
 3. Christ's answer.

VII. The third trial.
 1. His vision.
  a. Greece ; Rome ; the Orient.
 2. The test. Compromise.
 3. Christ's answer.
  a. Margaret Fuller's motto: "To the best thou knowes be always true."

VIII. The fruits of victory.

Matt 16-23-22ff 26-37-42
Luke 18-19 22-28.
Beecher's chap on Temptation ark 1-

LECTURE XI.

THE DISCIPLES.

Introduction : Compare with other teachers. Use of disciples.
I. The Baptist's testimony.
  1. The "Lamb of God."
  2. Result of John's testimony.
II. Eurekamen! (Matt. x, 2–4.)
  1. Andrew. (J. i, 37–39.)
  2. John. (Matt. iv, 21.)
  3. Peter. (J. i, 41.) Change of name.
  4. Philip. (J. i, 43.)
  5. Nathanael. (Bartholomew.) (J. i, 45–49.)
  6. James. Brother of John. (Matt. iv, 21.) Son of Zebedee.
  7. Matthew. Levi. (Matt. ix, 9.)
  8. James.
  9. Jude. (Thaddæus. Judas.) Son of Alpheus. Brother of Jesus.
  10. Thomas.
  11. Simon Zelotes. Zealots.
  12. Judas Iscariot.
III. Call to discipleship gradual.
IV. Character of disciples.
  1. Chosen chiefly from Galilee.
  2. From common people.
  3. Not deep spiritual natures.
  4. The inner circle. (Farrar, Life of Christ, 117–118.)
V. Nathanael's question. (For question and answer see Farrar, 71.)
VI. Tests.
  1. Of discipleship. "Follow me."
  2. Of authority. "Come and see."
VII. The contagion of life.

Questions.
  1. What element of weakness in John the Baptist's reformation?
  2. In what degree were the temptations of Jesus typical of tests which may come to any character?
  3. What is temptation? Has it any beneficent result?

Isaiah 53. [Messianic chapter]

Luke 18 chapter - vol 1.

[Born ...... disciples] -

___

Religion has two elements.
 Man element.
 God   "
God { faith - metaphysic, worship -
Man. { [Reason] - [cannot prove thee by reason]
       { [....] science of [......] -
       { Service.

One man, no man -

LECTURE XII.

CANA. CAPERNAUM. JERUSALEM.

A. Cana.
    I. The wedding feast. (J. ii, 1-11.)
        1. Cana of Galilee; location (?); home of Nathanael.
        2. A Jewish wedding.
        3. The guests. The feast.
        4. More abundant life.

B. Capernaum.
    I. Study the geography of the region around Sea of Galilee. (See Camb. Bib., Matt. 49.)

C. The cleansing of the Temple. (J. ii, 13-25.)
    I. The feast of the Passover. (Apr. ? 27 A. D.)
        1. The money changers.
        2. Traffic in sacrificial animals.
        3. The temple bazaars. The "ring" of the House of Annas.
    II. The Lamb aroused.
        1. Compare John and Jesus.
        2. Begins public career by an act of defiance.
        3. The whip of cords.
    III. The destruction of the Temple.
        1. "You are destroying this Temple and I will build it again."
        2. The rebuilding of the Temple.
    IV. The challenge.
        1. Priest and people.
        2. The courage of the critic.

Plan of Temple — Smith's Bible dictionary

LECTURE XIII.

CHRIST AND NICODEMUS.

I. The results of the temple cleansing.
   1. Opposition.
   2. Questions.
II. The heresy of Jesus.
   1. Heresy the conflict of life with opinion. "A taking for one's self."
   2. Two ways of committing heresy.
       a. Fighting fire with fire — bigotry with bigotry.
       b. Living. Life always in conflict with philosophy. The true follower of Christ always a heretic.
   3. Our attitude toward orthodoxy.
       a. Respect when we speak; deference when we judge. It is the opinion of the many.
       b. Indifference when we act. Our ideals are within, not without.
III. Nicodemus. (J. iii, 1-15.)
   1. A sanhedrist; a pharisee.
   2. His character.
   3. Subsequent history. (J. vii, 50-52; ix, 39.)
IV. Is religion a system of doctrines or a life?
   1. The (implied) question of Nicodemus: "What new doctrine have you to teach?"
   2. The hunt for new doctrines.
   3. Christ's answer, v. 3. Not new doctrines, but new life.
V. Regeneration.
   1. Jewish ideas concerning it.
   2. Christ's teaching it.
   3. Christian ideas concerning it.
   4. Like begets like.
VI. Spirit of skepticism. Illustrated. How met.
VII. The spiritual in religion.
   1. Rationalism and spirituality.
   2. The ignorance of the wise.
   3. The enemies of Christ's teaching.
       a. Ecclesiasticism substituting ceremonialism for worship.
       b. Traditionalism substituting opinion for life.

LECTURE XIV.

SYCHAR.

(John iv, 5–42.)

I. Samaria: location; people; temple; worship; relations between Samaritans and Jews.

II. Sychar: location; Jacob's well. (Gen. xxxiii, 18–20.)

III. The woman of Samaria: her character. Christ's treatment of outcasts.

IV. Christ as a conversationalist.
   1. He worked with individuals more than assemblies.
   2. Compare with other teachers.
   3. His method illustrated.
   4. His sympathy. What is tact?
   5. His power of drawing out.
   6. His spirituality.
   7. Always master of the conversation.

V. The lessons of the incident.
   1. The water of life.
   2. The way out of controversy.

VI. His assumption of the Messiahship.

VII. The wonder of the disciples.
   1. A woman.
   2. A Samaritan.
   3. An audience of one.

Questions:
   1. What gave Christ his power over the traders in the temple?
   2. Does the breaking up of theological systems indicate a decline of religion?
   3. What is orthodoxy? Consider the student's relation to it.

LECTURE XV.

THE RETURN TO GALILEE.

(J. iv, 43-54 ; Lk. iv, 14-23.)

I. The change in the home atmosphere. The Galileans received him.

II. The nobleman's son.
 1. The prayer and its answer.
 2. From sight to insight.
    a. Faith defined.
    b. Two kinds illustrated.
 3. The external Christ.
 4. Signs and wonders no basis of faith.

III. Christ's definition of his mission.
 1. Character of his preaching.
    a. Simple and powerful.
    b. In the vernacular of the common people.
    c. Always elevating and spiritual.
    d. No eloquence or rhetoric.
    e. Not scholastic or priestly.
 2. Condition of his audiences.
    a. Government despotic.
    b. Labor enslaved.
    c. Masses hopelessly ignorant.
    d. Scribes in place of prophets.
    e. Taxation was robbery.
    f. Stupor of hopelessness.
    g. The Golden Age behind.
 3. His message. (Lk. iv, 18-19.)
 4. Rejected by the Nazarines. (Lk. iv, 24-30.)

IV. The change contemporaneous with the growth of Christianity.

V. "By their fruits ye shall know them."

LXI of Isaiah

LECTURE XVI.

OPENING OF THE GALILEAN MINISTRY.

(Matt. iv, 12-25; Mk. i, 14-45; ii, 1-12; Lk. iv v.)

I. The enjoyment of success.
   1. Rejected at Jerusalem and Nazareth. Received at Sychar and Capernaum.
   2. The power and duty of sympathy.

II. The reception at Capernaum.
   1. Men of Galilee: honest, simple, impulsive, open-minded, and impressible.
   2. Men of Jerusalem: self-seeking, sophistical, critical.
   3. Dangerous use of criticism.

III. The fishermen of Galilee.
   1. Peter and Andrew; James and John.
   2. Christ's first pulpit.
   3. The lesson of the breaking net.

IV. The final call of the disciples.
   1. Fishers of men.

V. In the synagogue.
   1. Christ's sermons.
   2. He spoke with authority and not as the scribes.
   3. The appeal to conscience instead of precedent. (Read Geikie, Life of Christ, II, 3-4.)

VI. The treatment of the lunatic: contrast with the custom.

VII. Demoniacal possession.
   1. How regarded by the Jews; treatment.
   2. Suggested explanations.

VIII. Peter's home: health for activity.

IX. Sabbath evening: his work and rest.

Study IV and V chapter of Luke.

LECTURE XVII.

THE SABBATH.

(J. v, 1–47; Mk. ii, 23; iii, 6.)

I. The incidents.
  1. The pool of Bethesda, its legend.
  2. The corn-fields; the Sabbath for man.
  3. The withered hand; lawful to do good.

II. Elements of hostility to Jesus.
  1. Set himself against established order in church and state.
  2. Undermined the religious forms of the day.
  3. Attacked race-prejudice.
  4. Summary: race-pride, theological prejudice, superstitions, reverence, organized selfishness. These always the foes of Christ.

III. The Sabbath.
  1. Its origin.
  2. Laws do not originate in commandments, but commandments in laws.
  3. Early idea of the Sabbath.
  4. The Sabbath of the Pharisees.
  5. The Puritan Sabbath.
  6. Sabbath and Sunday; historical connection.

IV. Christ and the Sabbath.
  1. The protests against the social aspects. (Lk. xiv, 1–7 and 12.)
  2. The Sabbath made for man.
  3. Went to the synagogue.
  4. Rebuked legalism.

V. What shall we do with Sunday?
  1. How good must I be, or how good can I be?
  2. Sunday study.
  3. Sunday work.
  4. What shall we make others do?

(Read the Sermon on the Mount as preparation for next lecture.)

LECTURES XVIII–XX.

THE SERMON ON THE MOUNT.

(Matt. v–vii; Lk. vi, 20–49.)

I. Object of the discourse.
   1. An inaugural address.
   2. A setting forth of the new kingdom
   3. Not the sum of the gospel teaching.
   4. Not to give a set of rules for life.
   5. To create an appetite for righteousness.

II. Contrast with Sinai; with rabbinical teachings.

III. The plan of the sermon. Theme: the Kingdom of God.
   1. v, 3–16. The character of true disciples.
      a. The beatitudes.
      b. Application to life.
   2. v. 17–48. The laws of Christ contrasted with laws of Moses.
      a. Murder.
      b. Adultery.
      c. Swearing.
      d. Retaliation.
      e. Relations with our enemies.
   3. vi, 1–34; vii, 1–6. Principles of Christ's kingdom contrasted with the practices of the Pharisees.
      a. Almsgiving.
      b. Prayer.
      c. Fasting.
      d. Fretting.
      e. Censoriousness.
   4. vii, 7–27. How to enter the kingdom.
      a. First condition: faith.
      b. Second condition: obedience.
      c. Warnings against false teachers.
      d. The test of true religion.

IV. The analysis of the sermon.
   1. The beatitudes.

INNER LIFE — TOWARD GOD.	OUTER LIFE — TOWARD MEN.
1. The poor in spirit.	
2. They that mourn.	3. The meek.
4. They that hunger.	5. The merciful.
6. The pure in heart.	7. The peace-makers.
8. Persecuted for righteousness sake.	
The salt of the earth.	The light of the world

Matt V, VI, VII.

Distinguishing character of Sermon
Is it [...]
[...] realized;
[...]

[...] 252

THE LAWS OF THE NEW KINGDOM CONTRASTED WITH THE LAWS OF MOSES.

I. Not to destroy, but to fulfill.
   1. No repealing clause in the New Testament.
   2. Law regulates only external conduct.
   3. Laws are contemporary contrivances to run people who are without character. When character is developed the law is useless and becomes obsolete.
   4. Christ equally opposed to external legalism of the Pharisee and the spirit which makes his precepts the chief part of Christianity.
   5. Christ fulfilled in three ways.
      a. By spiritualizing.
      b. By showing the end of the law to be character, not conduct.
      c. By giving the power of obedience.
II. How is character to be attained?
   1. The common method.
   2. Christ's method. Except your righteousness exceed the righteousness of the scribes and Pharisees you cannot enter the kingdom.
      a. Principles, not forms.
      b. Love, not self-righteousness and pride.
      c. Moral righteousness, not ceremonial.
      d. Legalism can never be complete.
   3. Examples.
      a. Murder: thought as well as deed.
      b. Adultery: the wretchedness of evil in the heart.
      c. Swearing: only the man who respects himself can allow his *no* to stand alone.
      d. Retaliation.
      e. Relations with our enemies.

THE PRINCIPLES OF CHRIST'S KINGDOM CONTRASTED WITH THE PRACTICES OF THE PHARISEES.

I. Introductory. Negative and positive characters.
   1. Ethical systems contrasted with Christianity.
      a. The principle of non-interference.
   2. Christ's view of love.
      a. Egoism contrasted with altruism.

II. Doing right things from wrong motives.
   1. Externalism: a new name for an old sin.
      a. The man of the future: a creator, not a recipient.
   2. Moral counterfeiting: passing off our baser motives for our nobler ones.
      a. Life as a commercial transaction.
      b. "They have their reward."
   3. Almsgiving: our part of our gift is our motive; this only concerns us.
   4. Prayer. (See Lecture XXI.)
   5. Fasting: practices of the Pharisees.
      a. Christ's conflict with it.
      b. Matt. ix, 14–17.
      c. Joyousness of life.
      d. True and false fasting.
   6. The law of Christian reformation.
      a. Entire.
      b. Internal.
      c. The new life not patched on the old.
      d. The new spirit not contained in old forms.
      e. Fermentation.

III. Moral excellence contrasted with physical treasure.
      a. There is but one road to heaven for you, and that leads through your vineyard.

IV. Fretting. (Matt. vi, 19–34.)
   1. Care.
   2. Seeking first.
   3. Giving *versus* getting.

V. Censoriousness. (Read Beecher's Life of Christ, I, 353–363.)

LECTURE XXI.

CHRIST'S TEACHING CONCERNING PRAYER.

(Matt. vi, 5-15; vii, 21-27.)

I. Prayer customs among the Jews.

II. Christ's criticism. Ostentation defeats the object of prayer.

III. Christ's prayer.
    1. The address.
    2. The petitions.
    3. Its analysis.

IV. Our idea of prayer intimately connected with our idea of God.
    1. Does God change?
    2. Does man change?

V. Evolution of prayer in man.
    1. All centers in self.
    2. The recognition of two centers: God and man.
    3. God the center. "Thy will be done."
    4. Educational effect of prayer.

VI. Object of prayer. (Jordan, Evolution, bottom of page 59.)
    1. God's will (knowledge).
    2. Man's will (choice).
    3. "I will" (obedience).

VII. The idea of God.
    1. Immutable. Consistent with himself.
    2. Just. Impartial.
    3. Righteous.
    4. Omnipresent.
    5. This not always the idea of theology.

"When we have broken our god of tradition and ceased from our god of rhetoric, then may God fire the heart with his presence."—*Emerson*.

VIII. Some objections.
    1. Can not God overrule his own laws?
    2. Fatalism.
    3. God unapproachable.

IX. The active element in prayer.
    1. Matt. vii, 21.
    2. Prayer itself the chief agency for answering prayer.

X. Relation between our prayer and our knowledge.
    1. We can not pray beyond our belief.
    2. All prayer conditioned on faith.

Questions:
    1. In the light of Christ's teaching, what is character?
    2. Discuss the law hidden in Christ's figure, "New wine in old bottles."
    3. What is prayer?

LECTURE XXII.

THE CHRISTIAN CHURCH.

I. Introductory.
II. Definition of Christian church.
   1. Limitations of present discussion. (For full discussion see last lectures.)
III. The evolution of the church.
   1. Offshoots.
   2. Degeneration.
   3. Growth by successive explosions which burst through encrusted walls of form and precedent.
IV. The law of co-operation.
   1. Altruism and religion. (Jordan, Evolution, 64.)
V. The mission of the church.
   1. Christ's work. To do in a certain field what Christ did in Palestine.
   2. Negatively stated.
      a. Not to build a great organization.
      b. Not to worship.
      c. Not to be a school of philosophy, the guardian of a creed, the teacher of doctrine.
      d. These the means, not the end.
   3. The failure of formalism.
   4. Many-sidedness of love. The church of the future.
VI. The permanency and power of the church. What is back of it?
   1. Not due to fear and superstition.
   2. Not because of any particular creed.
   3. Not because of its wealth.
   4. Not any historic connection with the past.
   5. In the measure of Christ's spirit which it embodies.
VII. The secret of Christ's power.
   1. Identity of his will with God's will.
   2. The divine element.
VIII. Our relation to the church.
   1. Our relation to the work. Personal.
   2. Our relation to others. Social.

LECTURE XXIII.

SIGNS OF THE MESSIAH.

I. Closing words of the sermon. (Matt. vii. 21–29.)
    1. Hearing and doing.
    2. That part of our knowledge and our conviction which becomes action is permanent.

II. The effect of the sermon.

III. The period of popularity.
    1. A fascinating preacher.
    2. Joined religion and philanthropy.
    3. A man of the common people.
    4. Opposed to asceticism.
    5. A herald of freedom.
    6. New doctrines.

IV. The elements of his popularity also the elements of hostility. (See Lecture XVII, ii, 4.)

V. The signs of his messiahship.
    1. His works. Attitude toward the miracles.
    2. His words.
    3. His life. His life and personality the chief explanation of his works and words.

VI. The scientific test.
    1. The study of the records. A conclusion becomes
    2. A working hypothesis.
    3. The gospels re-read in the light of the hypothesis.
    4. The gospel definition of a miracle.

VII. Would not another do as well?
    1. Are we seeking a perfect being to worship or perfection in ourselves?
    2. The test of an ideal.

LECTURE XXIV.

TEACHING BY PARABLES.

(Matt. xiii, 1-53; Mk. iv, 1-34; Lk. viii, 4-18.)

I. Parables.
 1. Use by the Jews in teaching.
 2. Value as illustrations.
 3. Peculiarities of Christ's parables.
  a. Allegorical.
  b. Not applied.

II. Christ's reasons for using parables.
 1. His first teaching direct.
  a. Illustrate by Sermon on the Mount.
  b. This met with scorn and hardness.
 2. Mk. iv, 11. The question of the disciples and Christ's answer.
 3. Penal. Testing the disposition of those who listened.
 4. Sifting the fit from the unfit. In thought as well as brawn we are struggling for existence.
 5. Attractive and educational. A hold for memory.
 6. Disarming. The naked hook concealed.
 7. Always used on an unreceptive audience.

III. The evolution of the kingdom.
 1. The teachings of Christ best interpreted by using idea of growth as a clue.
 2. The kingdom does not come suddenly but gradually. Small beginnings. From low and simple to high and complex.
 3. The kingdom like a seed.
 4. Comes by human endeavor. (Parable of the sower.)
 5. Growth comes with opposition. (Parable of the tares.)
 6. Growth not to be measured by its small beginning. (Parable of the mustard seed.)
 7. Christ the disturber. Agitation a sign of life. (Parable of the leaven.)
 8. The end worth the cost. (Parable of the pearl of great price.)
 9. When and what is the harvest? (Parable of the net and fishes.)

Luke 7th v.
Matt. 12th v.

LECTURE XXV.

THE TRAINING OF THE DISCIPLES.

I. Was christ opposed to education?
    1. He did not attend any of the schools of his time. (Mk. vi. 2; J. vi, 42.)
    2. Criticised the schools and their teachers.
    3. His friends were largely ignorant men.
    4. His enemies were school men.
    5. Character of the schools of Christ's time.
        a. Classical; not practical.
        b. Developed the class, not the individual.

II. When is a man educated?
    1. "When he is good company for himself."—*Jordan.*
    2. When he is helpful.
    3. Failure of the rabbinical schools to do this.

III. Revolts against established systems always in the direction of more life.

IV. Christ's teachings the foundation of modern education.
    1. The Kingdom of God is within.
    2. Make the most of every man.

Here lies the key to the development of our public school, our social and political systems, and the unfolding protestantism of the age.

V. The preparation of the Apostles for their work.
    1. Both theoretical and practical.
        a. Their lecture course.
        b. Example of his life.
        c. Their experimental missionary circuit.
    2. The motive: compassion. (Matt. ix, 36.)
        a. The multitude: fainted (were harassed); scattered; no shepherd.
        b. The harvest plenteous, laborers few.

VI. The commission. (Matt. x, 1–15.)
    1. Begin at home.
    2. The message.
    3. The work.
        a. Healing, cleansing, life-giving.
        b. The institutional church.

VII. The call for workers.

LECTURE XXVI.

CHRIST IN JERUSALEM.

(The unnamed feast. John v.)

I. Signs of the coming storm.
   1. Suspicion, dislike, hostility, spies from Jerusalem.
   2. Murder of the Baptist.
      a. His last testimony concerning Christ.
      b. A prisoner of Herod Antipas. (Matt. xiv, 3–4.)
      c. Machærus.
      d. John's disciples visit Jesus.
      e. Herod's perplexity concerning John. (Mk. vi, 20.)
      f. The loyalty of John's disciples.
         [1] Like all "sects" they ended where their leader began.
      g. Christ's testimony concerning John.
      h. The feast and the dancers.
      i. The hasty promise fulfilled; would appear honorable to men, though unfaithful to himself.
      j. John's ghost in Herod's dreams. (Lk. ix, 7–9.)
      k. Effect of John's murder.

II. The unnamed feast at Jerusalem.
   1. Feast days among the Jews.
   2. Friends as well as enemies at Jerusalem.
   3. The journey probably taken alone.

III. The pool of Bethesda.
   1. The interpolated legend.
   2. The impotent man.
   3. A Sabbath-breaker.

IV. Heresy hunters.
   1. When the inner power and meaning of a religion are dead its forms are most prominent.
   2. When a religion has decayed in its spiritual life then is it most active and suspicious and tyrannical in its hunt for heresy.
   3. Examples from history.
   4. Heresy-hunting a sign of spiritual decline.

V. The results of the work.
   1. What law was broken?
   2. State's evidence.
   3. "They began to persecute Jesus."
VI. The rabbis rebuked.
   1. The man aroused.
   2. He assumes superiority.
   3. The three witnesses against them. (Farrar, Life of Christ, 176–179.)

LECTURE XXVII.

THE BREAK WITH THE PHARISEES.

I. Introductory.
  1. Security in obscurity.
  2. Security in popularity.
     a. Conformity and immortality. Spencer.
     b. Christ protected "for fear of the people."
  3. Danger in prominence.
     a. Christ's popularity rested largely on the excited wonder of an Oriental crowd.
  4. Danger in opposition.
  5. Nature puts a premium on prominence, on unlikeness, on contrariness, on individuality.
  6. Penalties for obscurity and conformity. "The obscure shall be more obscure." "To him that hath it shall be given."
  7. The leaders have always been martyrs.
     a. Darwin. Luther. Paul. Christ.
     b. The man who lives his life will always find his Calvary.
     c. The martyrs of yesterday the saints today.

II. Reasons for opposition of Pharisees. (Lecture XIII, viii; XVII, ii. Review.)

III. Opposition disguised, indirect, probably unorganized until after Bethesda.
  1. The incident at pool of Bethesda a critical point in Christ's life. (See Lecture XXVI; J. v, 1–47.)
  2. Public repudiation of Christ's claims by the authorities at the capital.
     a. Spies.
     b. Devices to entrap him. (Read J. v. 16 and 18.)
  3. Open hostilities. (J. v, 37–47.)

IV. Consciousness of impending doom.
  1. Change in Christ's attitude and speech.
  2. Return to Galilee. Murder of the Baptist. (Lecture XXVI, i.)
     a. Bethsaida Julias. Five thousand fed. Multitude would make him king.
     b. Disciples sent by boat to Capernaum. (J. vi, 1 21.)
     c. Jesus on the water. Peter's rash attempt. (Mk. xiv, 28.)

LECTURE XXVIII.

THE BREAD OF LIFE.

I. Introduction.
  1. The incident. (J. vi, 1-25.) 3. The discourse. (J. vi, 26-65.)
  2. The place — Capernaum. 4. Results. (J. vi, 66-71.)
II. The effect of the miracle.
  1. Instead of arousing understanding, it only made them long for more works.
    a. Loaves and fishes as bait to attract crowds.
    b. Nicholas Minturn. (Holland, 224 and 232.)
  2. The effect of the manna.
  3. The miracles seemed to be a stumbling block to the Jews.
  4. The real foundation of faith.
III. The sermon on the Bread of Life.
  1. Its figures. Common in Jewish literature. (Farrar, Life of Christ, 196.)
  2. Not lack of understanding, but lack of will.
  3. Much of teaching is testing.
    a. Objects.
      [1] To end the selfish hopes of the Jews.
      [2] To speak to the hating and materialistic Jews words they would not understand. (Lecture XXIV.)
      [3] To lead the disciples to a clearer understanding.
  4. The effect.
    a. Put an end to his popularity.
    b. Confirmed his conviction that the kingdom was not to be set up in his life-time.
    c. Private instruction to disciples.
IV. Meaning of the discourse.
  1. Disputes of theologians. (Ency. Brit., Eucharist, 653.)
    a. Were Christ's words to be taken literally? (J. vi, 49, 58, 63.)
    b. More than acceptance of his teaching.
    c. The completed metaphor.
      [1] Eating, digesting, assimilating.
    d. The spiritualized metaphor.
      [1] Transcendent influences of personality.
      [2] Interpretation of the figure.
      [3] The Kingdom of God, loyalty to God; inherited by living a life like Christ; the change internal; not power over men, but self-control; not new conditions of life, but new life.

LECTURE XXIX.

WHAT SHALL WE THINK?

(Matt. xv, 1-20; Mk. vii, 1-23.)
I. The appearance of the spies.
   1. Commissioned from Jerusalem.
   2. Their question. (Mk. vii, 2-5.)
II. The religion of ritualism.
   1. The Pharisee takes more pleasure in blaming another than in amending himself.
   2. The wail of ecclesiasticism. "Why walk not thy disciples according to the traditions of the elders?"
   3. Our relation to the past.
      a. Its use.
      b. Dangers of traditionalism.
III. Christ's analysis of ritualism. (Mk. vii. 1-23.)
   1. Its worship is vain; v. 7.
      a. True worship. Spontaneous; self-forgetful; natural.
   2. Its origin human; v. 8.
      a. Human opinions treated as divine laws.
   3. Displaces divine law by human ceremonies; vv. 9-13.
   4. Robs the individual of his freedom.
IV. The weapons of the Pharisees turned against themselves.
   1. Compare verses 2-5 with verse 8.
   2. The faults we see in others most often our own faults.
V. Concerning purity.
   1. The audience now the people; v. 14.
   2. Nothing that is, and remains external, defiles.
      a. Defilement internal.
      b. Vices (vv. 21-22) originate in the heart.
      c. Giving expression to evil thoughts confirms in evil.
VI. Thoughts concerning character building.
   1. We are what we think.
      a. Never on guard with ourselves.
      b. The habitual thought makes the man.
      c. If you would know yourself, look within.
      d. Our control of our thoughts.
      e. Our ideals the company we keep when we are alone.
      f. Sin breeds sin.
   2. The world what we interpret it.

(Read Farrar, Life of Christ, xxxi-xxxiii.)

Farrar page 333 - chap 31 -

LECTURE XXX.

THE PERIOD OF SECLUSION.

(Matt. xvi, 13-28; Mk. vii, 24-37; viii, 1-38.)
I. The nation not ready.
   1. A change in the plan of attack.
      a. No longer open warfare with great multitudes, but with the quiet leavening power of a few true lives.
   2. Avoids publicity. Hitherto he had ignored it.
      a. The blind man of Bethsaida. (Mk. viii, 22.)
      b. Secrecy enjoined. (Mk. vii, 36; viii, 26.)
      c. Taunted by his brethern for hiding. (J. vii, 2-5.)
II. Objects of the seclusion.
   1. He did not seek to preach but to rest.
   2. Uninterrupted conference with his disciples.
   3. He wished to make sure of his work before his enemies triumphed.
III. Tyre and Sidon. (Mk. vii, 24.)
   1. His fame had preceded him.
   2. Syro-phenician.
   3. His strange reply to her request. (v. 27.)
   4. Rebuked the narrowness of his disciples by seeming to partake of it.
IV. Decapolis.
   1. The deaf and dumb man. (Mk. vii, 32-37.)
   2. Christ's care to appear to use means.
V. Magdala. (Matt. xv, 39.) Dalmanutha. (Mk. viii, 10.)
   1. Sadducees and Pharisees united.
      a. The ruling classes.
          [1] Pharisees. Religionists.
          [2] Sadducees. Secularists.
          [3] Herodians. Romanists.
   2. They demand a sign. (Matt. xvi, 1-4.)
      a. His miracles not wonderful to them. They did not comprehend his life. They desired signs from heaven.
      b. The unrecognized signs.
   3. The woe of Chorazin and Bethsaida. (Matt. xi. 20.)
      a. The "sign" had been given, and had failed.
      b. The leaven of the Pharisees and Sadducees. (Mk. viii, 15.)
      c. The work in Galilee finished.

John 2-18
" 6-30
Matt 12-38

LECTURES XXXI-XXXII.

IS JESUS THE CHRIST?

(Matt. xvi, 13-28.)

I. Cæsarea. Philippi.
    1. Its temple on the rock. Dedicated to Cæsar. Worship of political power.
    2. Its sanctuary in the grotto. Dedicated to Pan. Worship of the forces of nature.

II. The incident.
    1. Deserted and a fugitive.
    2. All the Jewish conceptions of Christ had been shattered.
    3. Had the seed sprouted?

III. The momentous question. (v. 13.)
    1. The New Testament meaning of the term "Son of man."
    2. The answers of the multitude.
        a. John the Baptist.
        b. Elijah.
        c. Jeremiah.
        d. A prophet.
        e. No one saw in him the Messiah.
    3. Peter's answer. (v. 16.)
        a. The Christ. Peter's meaning.
        b. The living God — the Jewish figure.
    4. Christ's reply.
        a. Flesh and blood — a metaphor to denote man in contradistinction to God.
    5. The foundation of the church. (v. 18.)
        a. The spiritual union of God and man.
        b. Condition of membership. Faith in what Christ stood for.
        c. Condition of power. Faith in what Christ lived for.

IV. The promise of the key.
    1. The Jewish interpretation of Christ's figure.
    2. Christ's meaning.
        To my disciples (those who have chosen me as the ideal of their inner lives) I give the authority over their own spiritual lives, that they may no longer be bound by rules as the Pharisees, but shall bind and loose themselves as seems best to the spirit of liberty within.

V. The changing attitude toward religion.
  1. The old era of feeling — faith *versus* infidelity.
  2. The new era of thought — belief *versus* agnosticism.
  3. The part of modern science in this change.
     a. Overcome atheism.
     b. Inspired respect for mystery.
     c. The amount of mystery constant. (Herbert Spencer, Sociology.)
     d. Wavering faith in efficacy of natural selection.
        [1] Address of Salisbury before British Association.
        [2] Weismann's alternative.
  4. The growing power of the personality of Jesus.
     a. Dwarfing of sects.
     b. A factor in social problems.
     c. The effect on theology.
     d. Christ a fact of science.

VI. From the intellectual to the spiritual conception of Christ.
  1. The limitations of the intellect.
     a. Imposes its conditions on faith.
     b. "Faith is the synthesis of reason and spiritual approval."
  2. The spiritual faculty. Defined.
     a. Is this the same at the bottom as the intellect?
     b. Is the intellect at the bottom the same as the physical nature?
     c. These questions for psychology.
  3. The intellectual conception.
     a. The historical fact.
     b. The character.
     c. Comparative study of life and character.
     d. This the limit of the intellect.
  4. The added spiritual conception.
     a. The spiritual never can act without the intellectual foundation.
     b. The development of the spiritual conception.
     c. The answer to Christ's question really the attitude toward life.
  5. The cultivation of the spiritual life.

(Optional readings for controversies based on v. 18: Farrar, Life of Christ, 369–372; Geikie, Life of Christ, xlvi; Ency. Brit., art. Popedom; Ency. Brit., art. Catholic Church; Abbott, Com. Matt., 201.)

(See Outlook, April 21, 1894: Passing from Jesus to the Christ.)
(See Outlook, Oct. 6, 1894: Spiritual Life.)

LECTURE XXXIII.

SELF-SACRIFICE.

(Matt. xvi, 21–28.)

I. The work of Jesus half completed.
  1. The disciples knew him : the foundations laid.
    a. His remaining history must be studied in the light of this fact.
  2. He begins to foretell his own death.
    a. How did he know it ?
    b. Broken to them gradually.
    c. They could not comprehend.
      [1] New thoughts must always be collected in the garments of the old.
  3. Peter's misconception and rebuke. (vv. 22–33.)
    a. New life comes only through suffering and self-sacrifice.
    b. The Jewish conception of the Messiah involved the sacrifice of their enemies, not of themselves.

II. Christ's teaching concerning self-sacrifice.
  1. For whosoever will save his life shall lose it. He that findeth his life shall lose it. (Matt. x, 39.)
    a. First meaning: gaining this life loses the next. (J. xii, 25.)
    b. Second meaning: he that finds the lower sensual life loses the higher intellectual and spiritual.
    c. Third meaning : all self-seeking is self-losing.
      [1] He who seeks peace for himself loses it.
      [2] Self-forgetfulness a condition of happiness and success.
  2. Happiness.
    a. What is it ? Not intoxication, but life.
    b. Where is it ?
      [1] Child's way.
      [2] Solomon's way.
      [3] Christ's way.
    c. "Three-fold destiny." Hawthorne, Twice-Told Tales.
    d. Not in any external thing.

III. Altruism. The struggle for the life of others.
 1. A new chapter in the evolution of man.
 2. The physical basis: self-sacrifice in nature.
 3. The law of mutual aid as much a law as the law of mutual struggle.
 4. The two great factors in the evolution of man.
     a. Struggle for life.
     b. Struggle for the life of others.
     c. "But the greatest of these is love." (See Drummond, Ascent of Man.)

LECTURE XXXIV.

THE TRANSFIGURATION. DOCTRINE OF IMMORTALITY.

(Lk. ix, 28-36; Matt. xvii, 14-20, 22-27; II Pet. i, 16-18.)

I. The incident.
    1. Narrated by all the apostles.
    2. Time and place.
    3. Probable object.

II. Was it a dream?
    1. A concurrent dream as much a miracle as a supernatural visitation.
    2. Dangers of rational explanations.

III. Was it a legend?
    1. The time element.
    2. The intent of the narrators.

IV. The reality and character of the spiritual world.
    1. A common view. Death a long sleep.
    2. New Testament teaching concerning this point.
        a. Emphasis of spiritual detracts from importance of physical.
        b. No break in continuity of life.
        c. The physical body repudiated.
    3. Swedenborg's dream.
    4. Where is the abode of spirits?

V. Are there rational grounds for believing in immortality?
    1. Any clear, accurate, and definite conception of the spiritual world impossible.
    2. The pictorial teaching of the Bible concerning incomprehensible realities.
    3. Do we know things we can not demonstrate?
        a. The allegory of the worm.
    4. Universal belief.
    5. Personal conviction.
    6. Effect of belief in immortality on living.
    7. This doctrine the central teaching of Christianity.
        a. Secondary nature of body and mind.
        b. The ego.

VI. Conclusions from Christ's teachings.
   1. The spiritual existence is real.
   2. The judgment day is now.
   3. The spiritual world is very close.
VII. Dangers of spiritualism.
   1. Earthly activities forsaken for dreams.
   2. Spiritual ecstasy no substitute for practical duty.

LECTURE XXXV.

THE PARABLES OF THE LOST.
(Lk. xv, 1–32.)

I. Perea.
   1. Its location, ruins, population.
   2. Time, uncertain chronology.
   3. Ministry in Perea.

II. The first parable: The lost sheep.
   1. Lost to society.
   2. Individualism developed through society.
      a. The race a partnership.
      b. Human life impossible without society.
      c. Industrial and political organizations.
      d. The individual must serve the organization, or disintegration follows.
   3. The heart of all organization is loyalty.
      a. Loyalty implies:
         [1] Freedom.
         [2] Subserviency
      b. Society is the voluntary cooperation of free men for the common good.
      c. The paradox of liberty: only that man is free who willingly serves.
         [1] Not the man who does as he pleases.
         [2] Not the man who makes others serve him. "He who binds chains on a slave fastens the end around his own neck."
   4. Application of this principle.
      a. To the family.
      b. To government.
      c. To industry.
   5. Conclusions.
      a. A man serves himself who serves others.
      b. Cooperation a cure for social disorders.
      c. Foundation of cooperation.

III. The second parable: The lost coin.
   1. Lost to God.
   2. My kingdom or thy kingdom.
   3. Consequences of self-will.

IV. The third parable: The lost man.
    1. Lost to himself.
    2. His power no longer useful.
    3. Abuses of good.
        a. Appetite.
        b. Ambition.
        c. Acquisitiveness.
        d. Love.
        e. Conscience.
    4. The remedy of the parable.

LECTURE XXXVI.

THE GOOD SAMARITAN.

(Lk. x. 25-37.)

I. The incident.
    1. The lawyer.
    2. Self-righteous.
    3. Put the new teacher to the test.
    4. Self-contemplation.
    5. Judged by his own standard.
    6. Knowledge and action.
    7. The desire to get away from the personal and practical to the theoretical and abstract.

II. The parable.
    1. An illustration of the law of love.
    2. Jerusalem to Jericho. "The bloody way."
    3. Robbers of Palestine.
    4. The priest.
        a. Mercy commended by the law.
        b. A theological specialist. (Ex. xxiii, 4-5.)
    5. The Levite.
        a. A mimic of authority.
        b. Looked, moralized, departed.
    6. The law has no cure for suffering.
    7. The Samaritan.
        a. A mongrel — unclean and despised.
        b. Christ's reason for introducing him.

III. The greatest heresy is the lack of love.
    1. Philanthropy the heart of Christ's religion.
    2. Love for God means love for man.
    3. Why is there a gap between the church and the slums?

IV. My neighbor.
    1. Love has no neighborhood.
    2. Help those nearest. The stratification of society.

V. Our duty to the other half.
    1. The pity that shuns misery.
    2. Investigation.
    3. True philanthropy involves sympathy.

VI. The clannishness of the cultured.
  1. The meaning of brotherhood.
  2. The struggle for existence and the effect of isolation.
VIII. Going and doing.
  1. Life answers the questions we would stop to ask.

LECTURE XXXVII.

INCIDENTS FROM LUKE.

(Lk. viii, 4-18 ; ix, 46-62 ; x, 1-24, 38-42.)
1. The parable of the sower.   (Lk. viii, 4-18.)
    1. Christ's object.   "Take heed how ye hear."
    2. The word of God.
    3. Sown on all alike.
    4. The life of the seed depends on :
        a. Its reception.
        b. Its rooting.
        c. Its cultivation.
    5. The unfruitful hearers.   Three groups.
        a. Hear but heed nothing.
            [1] Hear but do not apprehend the truth.
            [2] Hindered at beginning.
            [3] The seed does not spring at all.
            [4] Have no life.
            [5] Illustrated by the Pharisees.
        b. Heed but resolve nothing.
            [1] Apprehension : transient, emotional.
            [2] Germinate the seed but die before opposition.
            [3] Enthusiastic beginnings.
            [4] Life superficial.
            [5] Illustrated by the Galileans.
        c. Resolve but do not persist.
            [1] Choked by care.
            [2] Death without fruit.
            [3] Life diverted, not centered.
            [4] Illustrated by Judas.
    6. Cause and cure.
        a. Careless hearing, wandering thoughts, hardened hearts.
            [1] Can we keep ourselves open-minded ?
        b. Mistaking emotion for principle.
            [1] Count the cost.
        c. Division of our energies.
            [1] We get that which we seek first.

II. Who is the greatest?
  1. The road to honor is humility. (Lect. XXXIII.)
  2. As a little child.
    a. Humility not thinking meanly of one's self, but not thinking at all of one's self.
III. With Christ and against Christ. (Lk. ix, 49-50.)
IV. Refused by the Samaritans. (Lk. ix, 51-56.)
  1. The office of Christianity wholly remedial, not punitive.

LECTURE XXXVIII.

CHRIST'S TREATMENT OF THE FALLEN.

(John viii. 1-11.)
I. Application of Christian principles to social problems.
II. The incident: the woman and her accusers.
    1. The arrest — according to Mosaic law.
        a. A dead letter among the Jews.
    2. The feast of tabernacles. A vintage festival.
    3. The spirit of the accusers.
        a. Not the spirit of sincere and outraged purity.
        b. The morals of the nation utterly corrupt.
            [1] This while their knowledge of the law nearly perfect.
            [2] Learning often linked with immorality
        c. They saw only an opportunity to entrap him.
        d. Ignored the torture of publicity.
        e. The accomplice.
        f. Contempt for public morality.
            [1] The temple court in Christ's time.
            [2] The open court and free press of today.
    4. The dilemma.
        a. Christ's popularity rested largely on his freedom from caste.
        b. If he acquitted the woman he would be a heretic.
        c. If he condemned her he would shock the multitude who had been attracted by his tenderness.
        d. If she was stoned he would be liable to arrest for stirring up a mob.
    5. The solution.
        a. He stopped and wrote to attract attention from the woman.
        b. They pressed upon him.
        c. "Let him that is without sin among you first cast the stone."
            [1] Not an abrogation of the law.
            [2] From the forum of law to that of conscience. (Rom. ii. 1-3.)
            [3] "Misery and mercy alone together."
        d. "Go and sin no more."

III. Christ's attitude toward sin.
   1. Recognized difference between sin and the sinner.
   2. A reformed sinner better than a dead one.
   3. Christianity remedial, not punitive.
IV. Is Christianity opposed to nature?
   1. The law of sowing and reaping.
   2. Indulgences.
   3. Forgiveness and penalty.
   4. Nature's cultivation and care for the remnant.
V. Effect on the prison system; on the pulpit; on society.

LECTURE XXXIX.

THE PRODIGAL.

(Lk. xv, 10-32.)

I. Remarks on the phrases of religion.
   1. Incomprehensible to many who use them.
   2. A real truth hidden by each one.
   3. Our effort to translate the terms of theology into the language of today.
   4. The hunger for a reason due to the wide-spread popular education.
   5. Men reject the terms which are empty, not the truth.
   6. Many have the truth who have rejected the terms.

II. Value of the parable to dissipate theological fog.
   1. We become our own interpreters.
   2. When striving to achieve belief without facts a parable brings them before us.

III. Evangelium in evangelio.

IV. Comments on the parable.
   1. The two sons.
      a. The elder: a pharisee, self-satisfied, proud.
      b. The younger: a sinner, self-abased, penitent.
   2. The demand.
      a. Illegal and unfilial.
      b. Independence of relationship to God and man.
   3. The division.
      a. The free will.
      b. Depravity cured by experience, not by law.
   4. The departure.
   5. The far country.
      a. Change accelerated under new conditions.
   6. The scattered and wasted life.
   7. The famine.
   8. The swine-herd.
      a. The lowest occupation a Jew could choose.
      b. An effort at reformation.
   9. Love and sympathy wanting.
      a. Reformation impossible in an empty heart.

10. He came to himself.
    a. Sin abnormal.
    b. The sane man commits no sin.
11. Repentance.
    a. Its definition and scope.
12. Forgiveness.
13. Restoration.
    a. The meaning of the symbols.
14. Pharisaic reception of the penitent.

Questions:
1. Was the prodigal as well off as if he had never gone into the far country?
2. Are "wild-oats" valuable as an experience?
3. Is the message of Christianity strengthened or weakened by the qualifications of Lect. XXXVIII. iii and iv?

LECTURE XL.

THE POOR RICH MAN.

(Lk. xii, 13–21.)

I. Christ not a law giver.
  1. The relation of the church to secular life.
    a. Not a court of law.
    b. Evils external and internal arising from the usurpation of this function.
    c. To fit men to settle their own disputes.
  2. Christ a teacher, not a judge.
    a. A judge decides for men — controls their wills.
    b. A teacher fits men to judge — makes men independent.
    c. How can we best help men?
      [1] By doing for them, or helping them to do?
      [2] By giving money, or work?
      [3] By deciding questions for them, or helping them to decide?
        Note.— The substitution of our energy, or judgment, or will, for another is a concession to human weakness, and should always be viewed with regret.
      [4] The misuse of Christ, the Bible, and the Church in this respect.

II. Christ's attitude toward riches.
  1. The rich fool. The rich man and Lazarus. (Lk. xvi, 14–31.) The rich young man. (Lk. xviii, 18–27.)
  2. A misconception growing out of the literal acceptance of the Bible.
  3. The danger of covetousness. (Lk. xii, 13–21.)
    a. A deteriorated moral sense.
      [1] Possession more than character.
    b. Materialistic ideals.
      [1] True and false riches. (v. 15.)
    c. The follies of the wealth-seeker.
      [1] Hoards instead of using.
      [2] Anticipates life but not death.
      [3] Would satisfy his soul without soul food.

4. The danger equal no matter what the thing coveted.
    a. 'Having instead of being.
    b. For self instead of others.
    c. Moral cannibalism.
5. Rich toward God. (v. 21.)
    a. The son of God must be god-like.
        [1] A god alone can comprehend a god. (Young. Night, ix, 835.)
    b. Power of enjoyment from self.

LECTURE XLI.

THE LABORERS.

(Matt. xx, 1-16.)

I. The story and its parallel.
II. Two classes of workers.
    1. Those who bargain. The hireling.
    2. Those who work for work's sake.
III. The call for work.
    1. Laid upon all life.
    2. Necessary to health, comfort, and existence.
        a. Idleness. Its penalties.
        b. Activity more essential than accumulations of its fruits.
        c. We learn far more through activity than through meditation.
    3. Christ's three degrees of excellence.
IV. The bargaining spirit.
    1. In life.
        a. How much am I worth? or,
        b. What am I?
        c. Work the means; the end not enjoyment or position but the man.
    2. In ethics and religion.
        a. He who does good because it pays may not be good.
        b. Bargaining prevents being.
        c. This spirit a survival.
V. The internal standard.
    1. Nature makes of each being a special creation.
        a. Each has its own environment, standard, rewards, and destiny.
        b. We are measured by ourselves.
            [1] Not by our wages but what we can make of them.
            [2] Not by our positions but what we can do in them.
        c. We can not be alike or like any one.
        d. Laws producing variation turn us back upon our peculiarities.
        e. Advantages of variety.
        f. Differences in capacity but no difference in opportunity.
        g. There is but one of you — what are you to make of him?

LECTURE XLII.

THE RESURRECTION OF LAZARUS. CHRIST'S TEACHING CONCERNING IMMORTALITY.

(John x. 1–54.)

I. Significance of this miracle.
   1. Regarded by friend and foe as the climax of the works of Jesus. (Spinoza.)
   2. Most startling and unnatural of the miracles.
   3. Attitude of the intellect.
      a. Belief and judgment.

II. Rationalistic attempts at explanation.
   1. It grew as a myth. (See Strausse, Life of Jesus.)
      a. Demands of the mythical theory.
      b. Latest opinions concerning John's Gospel.
   2. Was invented by John (as a parable) to illustrate a doctrine.
   3. The death of Lazarus was apparent, not real.
      a. Invented by the friends of Jesus.
      b. Jesus a fanatic. (Renan.)

III. Characteristics of John's narrative.
   1. He speaks as an eye-witness to certain events.
   2. He draws no conclusions, expresses no opinions.
   3. Reasons for the silence of the other writers. Fear of the authorities.

IV. Belief in immortality.
   1. Its developments. (See Clark, Ten Great Religions, II, xi.)
   2. Jewish doctrine.
      a. Did not assuage the present fact of death. (Munger. Freedom of Faith, 276.)
      b. Jesus modifies Jewish doctrines. (Read Munger. 258–9.)
   3. Science and immortality. No proof, no barrier. Agnostic.
   4. Nature and human life. Intimations. Suggestions.
   5. Reason as the basis of faith.

V. Christ's teaching.
  1. Death is sleep. (v. 11.)
  2. Himself the resurrection.
      a. Meaning of the figure.
      b. Is this to be taken as a promise merely?
  3. An assimilating faith in Christ leads away from death toward life.
      Note. — No one can live as Jesus lived toward men and toward God without sharing his attitude toward life and death.
VI. The Pharisaic creed contrasted with the faith of Jesus. (vv. 23–27.)
      a. Christ's indignation at human falsehood. (vv. 33–38.)
      b. Christ's sympathy.

LECTURE XLIII.

THE LAST JOURNEY.

I. Beginning of the end.
   1. In retirement at Ephraim. (J. xi, 54.)
      a. The council and plan of the rulers. (J. xi, 47-57.)
   2. What had been accomplished?
      a. He had preached in Galilee.
      b. The mission of the Twelve.
         [1] His Gospel too catholic for the Galileans.
         [2] His doctrine of self-sacrifice not attractive.
      c. Abandoned by the Galileans.
      d. He had preached in Judea.
         [1] His truth called heresy.
         [2] Rejected by the rulers.
      e. He had preached in Perea.
         [1] The mission of the seventy.
         [2] Transient interest only.
      f. The time of instruction now past.
         [1] It looks like failure.
         [2] The seed was sown.
   3. Christ an enigma even to his disciples.
      a. His parables are taken literally; his plainest words misunderstood.
      b. Possessed by their own notions.
      c. Their fears and anticipations.
   4. Christ's voluntary choice of death.

II. Salome's request.
   1. They supposed him about to assume his kingdom. (Matt. xx, 20-28.)
   2. Attempt to over-reach the disciples.
   3. The struggle for position.
      a. Christ's teachings concerning it. (Lk. xviii, 14.)
      b. Application to life.
         [1] Does position come by planning or by growth?

III. Zacchaeus. (Lk. xix, 1-10.)
  1. Jericho: a city of priests and publicans.
  2. A momentary return of popularity.
  3. The publican in the crowd of Jews.
    a. A thief and renegade.
    b. Called from ridicule and hatred to appreciation and honor.
  4. The murmuring multitude.
    a. Social sinners in the best society.

IV. A lesson in reformation.
  1. Effect of Christ's words on Zacchaeus.
    a. Made him forget the jeering crowd.
    b. Honored by Christ he would respect himself.
    c. All that was base in him would have defied contempt or hatred or criticism.
    d. All that was noble and good was evoked by tenderness.
    e. Love unseals what contempt would close forever.
  2. Effect of appreciation or condemnation on a child.
    a. A child is a man who is frank.
  3. Should we criticise?
    a. Is it helpful or harmful?
    b. Can it be avoided?
  4. Overcome evil with good.

LECTURE XLIV.

THE TRIUMPHAL ENTRY.

I. Bethany: location: its home.
  1. The feast. (J. xii, 2.)
    a. Martha's part contrasted with Mary's.
      [1] The social lesson.
        [*a*] House-keeping and home-keeping.
        [*b*] Feeders and hosts.
      [2] The religious lesson.
        [*a*] He serves best who receives most
    b. The meditative and active should be combined. (Read Farrar, 461–462.)
  2. The annointing. (J. xii, 1–11.)
    a. Mary's motives and act.
      [1] Should this $300 have been given to the poor?
    b. Judas. His avarice.
      [1] Shown in his plans for the kingdom.
      [2] Communion with Christ a daily rebuke.
      [3] He found himself slipping through his disguise.
      [4] His pretended regard for the poor
      [5] Hypocrisy would contrast philanthropy and piety.
      [6] Christ's rebuke a final blow to his Messianic hopes

II. The betrayal.
  1. Judas attempts to save something from the wreck.
  2. His bargain with the chief priests.
  3. Continues with the disciples.

III. Palm Sunday. (Lk. xix, 28–48.)
  1. The contagion of enthusiasm.
  2. The growing procession.
  3. Hosannas and palm branches, then curses and the cross.
  4. Christ on the Mount of Olives. (v. 41.)

IV. Two views of the triumph.
  1. What the Jews saw.
    a. A king coming into his kingdom.
    b. The material supremacy of the Jew.
  2. What Christ saw.
    a. A nation blind to its own history.
      [1] The message of Israel.
    b. A people preparing their own destruction.
    c. Judaism must die in giving birth to Christianity.

LECTURE XLV.

EVOLUTION OF BELIEF.

I. Three epochs of modern thought.
  1. Age of controversy.
     a. Violent attacks and defense.
     b. Struggle inevitable.
     c. Results beneficial.
  2. Age of reconciliation.
     a. Mutual respect and concession.
     b. Period of compromise.
  3. Age of reconstruction.
     a. Magnification of man. Greater than anything he believes.
     b. How may science and religion be used in elevating man?
     c. Period of activity and life.
II. Value of criticism.
III. Our attitude toward new truth.
  1. No expression of truth final.
     a. A wider development sure.
  2. Danger of regarding the truth as final.
     a. Sceptics made by forbidding doubt.
     b. Result of checking desire for knowledge.
IV. Intellectual growth intermittent.
  1. Changes occur suddenly.
     a. Periods of preparation; gathering of material.
     b. Moments of interpretation and revelation.
     c. "We do not grow into new truths, we awake to them."
  2. We should be both alert and passive.
     a. Passive to the spirit of truth.
     b. Alert to the unfolding revelation.
V. Truth no fixed form.
  1. Change not in it but in us.
  2. Not a revelation from God, but
  3. A revelation of God.
     a. Here is the key to the study of the Bible, of church history, of Christ, and of nature.

VI. Some vehicles of truth considered.
    1. Trinity.
    2. Atonement.
    3. Sin.
    4. Retribution.
    5. Inspiration.
    6. Christ.

VII. In other's shoes.
    1. Our attitude toward the belief of others.
    2. Our old clothes may be worn by another with comfort.
    3. Ridicule ridiculous.
    4. Charity always profitable.

LECTURE XLVI.

THE GREEKS.

(John xii, 20-36.)

I. The second cleansing of the temple. (Matt. xxi, 10-13.)
   1. Why necessary the second time.
      a. The lessons of history.
   2. Christ's ideal of a temple.

II. The wondering Greeks.
   1. Attracted by the unusual enthusiasm.
   2. Greek philosophy eclectic.
      a. Religious systems studied to add to their philosophy.
      b. A good way to understand religion, but not to become religious.
         [1] Philosophical living.
         [2] Ready-made theories of life do not always fit the conditions.
         [3] Learn to do by doing.
   3. Christ evidently rebuffs these inquirers.
   4. His prophetic interpretation of the incident.
      a. The united race.
      b. Do we see it coming?
      c. Are Christ's teachings the cause?

III. Life conditioned.
   1. What follows is a condemnation of Hellenism.
      a. Grecian civilization is human life cultivated from the view point of enjoyment and withdrawn from self-sacrifice.
   2. Self-sacrifice symbolized. (v. 24.)
   3. A universal law.
      a. Most important in nature.
         [1] Her care for the future.
      b. Spiritual life only through sacrifice.
   4. Hatred of lower life a safeguard against it. (v. 25.)

IV. Christian service.
   1. In what it consists. (v. 26.)

V. A glimpse into Christ's secret life. (vv. 27-28.)

VI. The cross of Christ.
   1. Judges the world.
   2. Attracts the world.

VII. The way out of perplexity. (vv. 34-36.)
   1. Walk as ye have the light.
   2. In activity is knowledge, power, happiness, and honor.

LECTURE XLVII.

THE CHALLENGE.

(Matt. xxi, 23-46.)

I. The attack on Christ.
    1. His authority questioned.
        a. The innovations of Christ's teaching undermined the authority of the priests.
        b. The ecclesiastical assumption of authority.
        c. Variance between ecclesiasticism and religion.
    2. "What was the authority of John the Baptist?"
        a. The dilemma. (vv. 25-26.)
        b. Religious investigation often veils hypocrisy.
    3. What is the test of authority in religion?
        a. The test of appointment.
        b. The test of fruit.

II. Christ's defense.
    1. His challenge to scribe and priest.
    2. Value of the parable in attack.
    3. Parable of the two sons.
        a. Profession.
        b. Practice.
    4. Parable of the rebellious husbandmen.
        a. Messengers from God.
        b. The doctrine of accountability not a theological doctrine only.
        c. The son rejected.
        d. National accountability.
        e. Use it or lose it.
    5. Parable of the wedding feast.
        a. Guilt and loyalty, individual and personal.
        b. The false friend.
        c. Application to the Jewish priesthood.
            [1] Professed loyalty of Jehovah but did not work righteousness.
            [2] Received the gifts of light and liberty and truth but shut out the pagan and gentile.
            [3] Formally perfect, inwardly vile.
        d. To bad men nothing is so maddening as the exhibition of their own self-deception.

LECTURE XLVIII.

THE LAST DAY OF CONFLICT.

(Matt xxii, 15-46.)
I. Christ's behavior in the midst of enemies.
   1. His gentleness and meekness not the result of timidity and irresolution.
   2. He parries their blows, defeats them, and utters against them the most terrible philippic of literature. (Matt. xxiii, 1-39.)
   3. How would this seem in another man?
II. The strange allies.
III. The Herodians.
   1. Apostate Jews, politicians, Romanists.
      a. How regarded by the orthodox.
      b. Their attitude toward Christ.
         [1] A disturber of their peace.
         [2] A discerner of their motives.
   2. Their trap.
      a. A dispute, words of flattery. "Is it lawful to give tribute to Caesar?"
      b. The poll-tax.
      c. Their motives exposed.
      d. Christ's answer: "Give back to Caesar the things which are Caesar's."
         [1] Acceptance of gifts and favors demands loyalty.
IV. The Sadducees.
   1. The infidels and materialists of Palestine.
      a. Denied the resurrection and immateriality.
   2. They sought to vex and ridicule.
   3. Ignorance is not met with contempt.
   4. Question and answer. (Lk. xx, 34-36.)
   5. The problems of this world not to be solved in terms of the next.
V. The Pharisees.
   1. They had destroyed the simplicity of religion.
   2. They had divided Judaism into sects.
   3. To which denomination did Christ belong?
   4. Christ's answer seems to set aside all schools and sects.

IV. Christ questions his critics. (vv. 42–45.)
   1. Inconsistency of their conceptions of the Messianic Kingdom.
   2. He exposes their weakness before the multitude.
   3. They fear to question him more.

(Read Farrar, Life of Christ, li.)

LECTURE XLIX.

A PHILIPPIC.

(Matt. xxiii.)

I. The limits of mercy.
    1. Doctrine of retribution.
    2. When love pleads in vain, justice rules.
        a. Relation of love and justice.
            [1] Love does not hold justice in check.
                [*a*] It may in human affairs, never in divine.
                [*b*] Danger in the doctrine of punitive justice being opposed by love.
            [2] Justice and love coexist.

II. Reasons for Christ's rebuke.
    1. Attitude toward ignorance, humility, the depraved.
        a. The sinner knows that the way of the transgressor is hard. He does not know a better way.
        b. He needs hope, counsel, courage.
        c. To such Christ always reached the hand of help.
    2. He rebuked and unmasked the false witness.
        a. Those who thought they were virtuous because they were religious.
        b. Those who devoured widow's houses and prayed long prayers.
        c. Those who paid tithes but omitted mercy and righteousness.
        d. Those who spent all their zeal in making proselytes, and none in making character.
    3. The only cure for self-conceit is humiliation.

III. Pharisaism described.
    1. Burdensome and unsympathetic.
        a. Truth and falsehood in religion.
            [1] The false enact laws and bind burdens.
            [2] The true impart power.
        b. In so far as your religion is burdensome it is false.
    2. Ostentations.
    3. Factions.
        a. Christ forbids the exercise of spiritual authority over the conscience; or,
        b. The submission to it.

III, 4. A hindrance to religion.
    a. By denying freedom of thought.
    b. By preventing the truth
    c. By bad example.
  5. Proselyting. (v. 15.)
  6. Whitened sepulchres.

IV. The change from noble indignation to tender pity.
  1. "I would but ye would not."

LECTURE L.

THE END OF THE WORLD.

(Matt. xxiv.)

I. The attraction of this subject for the superstitious.
  1. Attempts to take literally the poetical expressions of the Bible.
  2. Attempts to decipher the future include ignorance of the present.
  3. No attempt to locate the coming of future events ever has or ever will succeed.
     a. This will not prevent people from trying.
     b. The mental characteristics which admit evidence for fulfillment of imagined prophecy preclude the admission of genuine testimony.
     c. Foundation of genuine prophecy.

II. Prophecy.
  1. We ignore here all prophecy not based on continuity.
  2. Objects of prophecy.
     a. To warn, to inspire hope, to incite to courage.
     b. To interpret the sequence of events.
     c. Never to emphasize chronological order or establish the absolute time of an event.
     d. Characteristic of men to emphasize c. more than a. and b.
  3. History is itself prophetic.
     a. The partial fulfillment becomes an historical prophecy of a further fulfillment.
     b. The lessons of the past.
     c. Cause and effect in Christ's view of Jerusalem.

III. The farewell to the Temple.
  1. The feelings of the disciples.
     a. National pride in the spot. (Farrar, 542.)
  2. The sadness of Christ.
     a. To him the beauty of the Temple was the sincerity of its worshipers.
     b. No glory of construction could change a den of thieves into a house of worship.
  3. The prediction.

IV. The question. (v. 3.)
  1. When?
  2. "Beware," "watch," "endure," "pray."
  3. False Messiahs.
      a. Wars and rumors of wars.
  4. Destruction of Jerusalem.
      a. Its relation to the foundation of the Christian church.
  5. The second coming of Christ.
      a. In process of fulfillment.
      b. Its relation to the foundation of the kingdom of God.

LECTURE LI.

THE LAST SUPPER.

(Matt. xxvi, 1–29. Read Farrar, liv.)

I. The conspiracy of Christ's enemies.
    1. All factions united.
    2. The palace of Caiphas. Tuesday evening.
    3. The incentive.
        a. Defeated and abashed in open encounter.
        b. In the scene of their highest dignity.
        c. In the presence of their most devoted adherents.
        d. Forced to confess their ignorance of scripture.
        e. The character of their assailant.
    4. The union.
        a. Pharisees, Sadducees, Herodians, priests, scribes, elders.
        b. An alliance of fanaticism, unbelief, and worldliness; the bigot, the atheist, the utilitarian.
    5. The verdict.
        a. Death.
        b. By subtlety, not by violence.
        c. Must be postponed until after the Feast.
            [1] It would pollute his executioners.
            [2] The crowd would be gone.
    6. Plans changed by Judas.

II. The quiet Wednesday and Thursday.

III. Thursday evening. (Lk. xxii, 14–27.)
    1. The strife for position.
        a. The law of service.
    2. Christ washes his disciples' feet. (J. xiii. 1–10.)
    3. Judas' presence prevents free conversation.
        a. Christ drives him from the room.
        b. His method. Protects Judas from the other disciples, yet shows him his purpose is known.

IV. The Supper.
    1. The Passover. Its ritual.
    2. New meaning given by Christ.
    3. Singular growths from a simple incident.
        a. Conditions imposed by theology on participants.
        b. Dogmas concerning it.
    4. A memorial.
    5. A parable.
    6. A prophecy.

i

LECTURE LII.

THE HEART OF CHRISTIANITY.

(J. xiv, 1–31.)

I. The last discourse. (J. xiii, 31 ; xvii, 26.)
  1. The Holy of Holies of the Bible.
    a. The words not to be understood by reason only.
    b. Two keys to unlock secrets of nature and of religion.
    c. Best commentary the personal life of the reader.
    d. Times when silence is the best method of study.

II. God in men.
  1. This the heart of Christianity.
  2. The highest point reached in the development of religion.
  3. The only conception of God that can be universal.
  4. The only rational conception.
  5. The human craving for incarnations, for concrete expressions of truth.

III. The disciples begin to comprehend.
  1. The shadow of the cross.
  2. Their materialistic conception of hades and a future life.
  3. Christ's hopefulness.
  4. This world not the only abode of living beings.
  5. Christ tests their understanding.

IV. The inquiring disciples.
  1. The perplexed Thomas. (v. 5.)
    a. The way to God ?
    b. *Ego sum via, veritas, vita.*
      [1] More important that they should know the way than the goal.
    c. "No man cometh to the Father but by me."
    d. Can we not by searching find out God ?
  2. Philip's question. (v. 8.)
    a. Did he wish that the heavens be rent asunder ?
    b. Many would have believed this.
  3. The difficulty of Judas Lebbaeus. (v. 22.)
    a. How can we see and others not see ?
    b. God lives with them that love Him.

1

LECTURE LIII.

THE PERPETUAL CHRIST.

(John xv.)

I. The doctrine of the Trinity.
   1. Its history.
   2. Church divisions concerning it.
   3. A doctrine that has nourished has its basis of truth.
   4. Men quarrel over dogma who agree in spiritual perception.

II. The basis of the doctrine.
   1. Held alike by both sides.
   2. The spiritual aspect. Three propositions
      a. God.
      b. Personal relation.
      c. Revelation.

III. How may one being reveal himself to another?
   1. Three channels:
      a. Intellect
      b. Sensibilities. (Abbott's illustration from Liszt.)
      c. Will.

IV. The intellectual revelation.
   1. From Herbert Spencer.
   2. The unity in history and humanity.
   3. Matthew Arnold.
   4. The One in the universe.

V. The moral revelation.
   1. Finite and Infinite.
   2. God in human terms.
   3. Christ a revelation.

VI. The ground of controversy.
   1. Miraculous birth.
   2. Life.
   3. Personality.
   4. Teachings.
   5. Miracles.
   6. Resurrection.
   7. Christianity.
   8. Divinity.

VII. The abiding Christ.
    1. God in humanity.
        a. Inspiring human experience.
        b. Speaking in human hearts.
        c. The comforter.

VIII. Harmful conceptions in Trinitarianism.
    1. The three gods joined in one.
    2. Doctrine of polytheism.
    3. These not the truth in Trinity.

IX. Harmful conceptions in Unitarianism.
    1. Life in three separate strands.
    2. These not the truth in Unity.

X. The interpretation of Christ.

LECTURE LIV.

GETHSEMANE.

(Matt. xxvi, 30–56; Mk. xiv, 33–50; Lk. xxii, 39–53; J. xviii, 2–12.)

Thursday midnight, April 6, to one o'clock Friday morning.

I. In the garden.
   1. A customary retreat; known to Judas.
   2. Gethsemane; oil-press.
      a. A grove of olive trees.
II. The double guard.
   1. Peter, James, and John.
   2. To protect against suprise. Themselves or him?
   3. The sleep of sorrow.
III. Nature of Christ's conflict.
   1. He was not a stoic.
      a. In proportion to his sympathy he suffered.
   2. Placid heroism.
      a. Contrast with Jewish heroes.
      b. A repressed conflict under the calm exterior of his life.
   3. Not elevated above the woes of humanity.
   4. To the prophetic eye the future more real than the present.
   5. In the prime of manhood, life before him, eager for work, conscious of capacity.
   6. The vicarious element.
   7. False friends.
   8. His submission voluntary.
   9. After all is said, mystery remains.
      a. No psychology can fathom Christ's experience.
      b. To unscarred youth Gethsemane will always be a mystery.
         [1] By our own Gethsemanes we will understand his trial.
         [2] They come to all who bear great thoughts.
IV. Christ's prayer.
   1. Was it possible for the cup to pass?
      a. By the abandonment of his life purpose.
      b. By falsehood to himself.
   2. He would not desert humanity.
   3. The struggle real but never doubtful.

V. Christ's answer to his prayer.
  1. "Thy will, not mine, be done."
  2. This more than resignation.
     a. Real prayer more than submission.
        [1] A man may be resigned to the inevitable.
        [2] Jesus prayed (desired) God's will to be accomplished.
     b. Prayer the voluntary execution of God's will by a free will.
  3. The battle of his life won in the garden.
VI. In the presence of danger.
  1. Might have escaped, leaving the disciples sleeping.
  2. Arouses them. Quietly warns them.
  3. Pushes to the front between them and danger.
  4. Judas.
  5. The crowd abashed.
  6. Peter fighting and Peter fleeing.
  7. Christ pleads only for his disciples.
  8. Deserted.

LECTURE LV.

BEFORE THE PRIESTS AND SANHEDRIN.

(Matt. xxiii, 57 to xxvii, 2 ; Mk. xiv, 53 to xv, 1 ; Lk. xxii, 54–76 ; J. xviii, 13–27.)

I. From Gethsemane to the Palace.
  1. Annas.
    a. The chief of the pontifical ring.
    b. Degradation of the high priest's office.
    c. Deposed but still in power.
      [1] Five sons in succession high priest.
      [2] Caiaphas his son-in-law.
    d. Farrar, Life of Christ, 598.
  2. The interest of Annas a proof that Christ had become a political figure.
    a. Afraid he would alienate the people from the priestly clique.
    b. Significant disappearance of the Pharisees.
  3. Caiaphas and the Sanhedrin.

II. The charge of blasphemy.
  1. Jewish law on the subject.
    a. See Ex. xx, 3–5 ; Deut. xiii ; xviii, 20.
    b. But one authorized equal of Moses. (Deut. xviii, 15–18.)
  2. Judge Greenleaf's opinion.
  3. Opinions of jurists.
    a. The form of trial illegal.
    b. His conviction substantially right in point of law.
    c. Citation II, 1, *b* (above) only ground for acquittal.
    d. Either must substantiate his claim of super-human character or stand convicted under Mosaic law.
  4. Christ seems with wise caution to have guarded against this hour of trial.
    a. His accusers could not array the evidence as we can.
      [1] No witness in support of Judas.
      [2] Their false witnesses did not agree.
    b. Even before a packed tribunal they could not secure conviction.

III. Jesus on the witness stand.
  1. Questioned concerning his disciple and doctrine.
  2. Points to his record. (J xviii, 19–20.)
  3. Is struck.

IV. Peter's denial
   1. Thrice repeated.
   2. Christ overhears the last and looks at Peter.
   3. Contrast between Peter and Judas.

V. The fearful judge and the dumb prisoner.
   1. Caiaphas was conducting an illegal trial.
   2. This made him tremble before Christ's silence.
   3. Mk. xiv, 60.
   4. The priest's question
      a. Christ asked to convict himself.
      b. The peculiar form of the question.

VI. Christ's "I am." (Mk. xiv, 62.)
   1. Why he could no longer keep silent.
   2. Quiet in the day of popularity.
      a. The declaration useful to him then.
      b. Now all must be lost.
   3. How are we to understand Christ's answer?

LECTURE LVI.

TRIAL BEFORE PILATE.

(Matt. xxvii, 15-31; Lk. xxiii, 6-12; J. xviii, 28-39; xix, 4-16. Farrar, Life of Christ, lx.)

I. Christ led to Pilate.
  1. Power of the procurator.
  2. Character of Pilate.
  3. His history.
  4. Reasons for his presence in Jerusalem.

II. Contest between unscrupulous persistence and cowardly compromise.
  1. The Jews knew how to conquer Pilate.
  2. The priests and the mob.
  3. The behavior of the prisoner.
  4. The scene.

III. The accusation.
  1. The call for the charge surprises them.
  2. They asked for license to kill. Pilate called for testimony.
  3. "If he were not guilty we would not have delivered him."
    a. Pilate knew the Jews too well to believe this.
  4. The charge of blasphemy would not hold in a Roman court.

IV. A new charge. (Lk. xxiii, 2.)
  1. Perverting the nation — i. e., from the Romans.
    a. Strange charge for Jews to make.
  2. Forbidding to give tribute.
  3. Saying he is Christ, a king.

V. Pilate assumes jurisdiction.
  1. The private examination.
    a. Silent before the Jews he speaks to the Roman.
    b. A king, but no preacher of sedition.
      [1] His accusers a witness to this fact.
    c. His kingdom not of this world.
    d. He came to witness for the truth.

VI. "What is the truth?"
  1. Pity and contempt.
  2. A Roman realist.
  3. A baseless vision of a religious enthusiast.
  4. Pilate gives his verdict.

VII. Jesus sent to Herod.
1. A master-stroke of policy.
2. Herod Antipas.
3. The second derision.

VIII. Back to Pilate.
1. Now was the time for Pilate to be strong.
2. Barabbas.
3. The warning of the dream.
4. "What then shall I do with Jesus?"
5. "Thou art no friend of Caesar's if thou let him go."
6. The hand washing.
7. "His blood be on thy hands."
    a. The revengers of history.
8. "And they took Jesus and led him away."

LECTURE LVII.

THE CRUCIFIXION

(Matt. xxvii, 32–56 ; Mk. xv, 20–47 ; Lk. xxiii, 26–56 ; J. xix.)
I. Intoductory ; varying views.
II. Crucifixion.
    1. Not a Jewish mode of punishment.
        a. Its infliction by the Romans a badge of Israel's servitude.
    2. Exposure of bodies. Mosaic law on the subject. (Deut. xxi, 22, 23.)
    3. Reserved by Romans for foreigners and slaves.
        a. Condemned by Cicero and others.
III. From judgment to execution.
    1. The procession.
    2. Simon the cross-bearer.
    3. The women of Jerusalem.
        a. The beginning of philanthropy
            [1] Born in the ostentatious grief of the age.
        b. "Weep not for me but for yourselves."
            [1] Christ not an object of pity.
                [*a*] He was winning the battle of his life.
                [*b*] He was true.
            [2] Spirit of the prohibition violated.
                [*a*] Dramatic oratorical portraitures of Christ's sufferings.
                [*b*] By much so-called sacred art.
            [3] "Christ would have been an object of pity had he from fear of death preferred a broken life."
            [4] The sad thought is the sin that crucified him.
        c. Refuses the stupefying drink.
IV. Golgotha (a skull) *Lt. calvaria.*
V. The gambling soldiers.
VI. The taunt of the priests.
    1. "He saved others ; himself he can not save."
    2. "Let him alone and see if Elias will come."
VII. The two thieves.
    1. One curses and reviles.
    2. One rebukes and prays.
        a. The hope in which Christ died.

1

VIII. The circle of friends.
    1. John and the mother of Jesus.
    2. Matt. xxvii, 55, 56.

IX. The darkness and the earthquake.
    1. Deserted.
    2. "It is finished."

X. The broken heart.
    1. Anticipated the death of the cross.

XI. The burial of Christ.

i

LECTURE LVIII.

THE RESURRECTION.

(Matt. xxvii, 57–66 ; Mk. xv, 42–47 ; Lk. xxiii, 50–56 ; J. xix, 38–42.)
(Matt. xxviii ; Mk. xvi ; Lk. xxiv ; J. xx, xxi.)

I. The story of the resurrection
  1. Condition of the disciples.
      a. Heart-broken.
      b. Had never understood his prophesies or parables.
      c. Without hope.
         [1] Had not anticipated a resurrection.
      d. Without faith.
         [1] "We had trusted that this had been he which should have redeemed Israel."
      e. Only love lived, and love without faith and hope is anguish.
  2. The women at the sepulcher
      a. Find the stone rolled away.
      b. An angelic messenger.
      c. Run to tell the disciples.
      d. They doubt.
  3. Peter and John are convinced.
      a. J. xx, 8, 9.
  4. Mary Magdalene.
      a. Thinks the tomb has been robbed.
      b. Sees and believes.
  5. The soldiers make their report.
      a. Are bribed.
      b. Their false story.

II. The perplexed disciples.
  1. Their attitude toward the resurrection.
  2. Insufficient evidence.
      a. Women's tales.
      b. Testimony of Peter and John negative.
      c. Peter more impulsive than judicial ; John visionary.
  3. Meet to discuss the situation.
      a. The secret meeting Sunday night.
  4. The two disciples from Emmaus.

III. Jesus appears in their midst.
   1. Calms their fears.
   2. Assures them that he is no apparition.
      a. Bade them touch him.
      b. Ate with them.
   3. Explains the meaning of his passion and death.
IV. Thomas.
   1. Not present at the first appearance.
   2. A natural unbeliever.
   3. Plenty of loyalty but no faith.
   4. Plain, practical, prosaic.
   5. Seeing was believing.
      a. In those days nothing was heresy but unfaithfulness.
   6. Convinced. Love won where argument failed.
V. Lessons of the resurrection.
   1. Continuity of life.
      a. This primary, the evidence and method subordinate.
   2. Leaving the main question to be settled in its own way, what did Christ teach concerning it?
   3. Examination of evidence.
      a. Universally believed by the early church.
      b. Sustained by four narratives.
      c. Precautions of the priests.
      d. Surprise of the disciples.
      e. Marvelous change in the demeanor of the disciples.
      f. The change in the Sabbath.
      g. It has worked well.

LECTURE LIX.

THE GREAT COMMISSION.

(Matt. xxviii, 18-20.)

I. Christ's definition of his mission. (Lk. iv, 16-21.)
II. His mission given to the church as its commission.
   1. His last command.
      a. "Go ye."
         [1] An aggressive religion.
         [2] Christianity the only missionary religion.
            [*a*] Imitators.
            [*b*] Christianity thrives only as a missionary religion.
            [*c*] The earth is not large enough to allow love and need to live in peace.
            [*d*] The Golden Rule makes meddlers.
      b. The doctrine of *laissez faire*.
         [1] Does the liberty we claim for ourselves and grant to others preclude our interference?
         [2] Christianity seeking and saving.
            [*a*] This because its centre is love.
         [3] Nothing else is Christianity.
            [*a*] Not high thoughts.
            [*b*] Nor lofty ideals.
            [*c*] Nor feeling high emotions about God or his works.
         [4] Religion consists less in forming ideals than in realizing them.
            [*a*] The intellectual substitute for religion.
            [*b*] Just as harmful as the emotional substitute.
            [*c*] Life realized not by knowledge nor by faith but by that which is the parent of both.
         [5] Emotion mistaken for religion.
            [*a*] This only religion when it leads to action.
            [*b*] The danger of undischarged feeling.
   2. Three degrees of discipleship.
      a. Following. (J. i, 43.)
      b. Appearing. (Matt. v, 16.)
      c. Going. (Matt. xxviii, 19.)

www.ingramcontent.com/pod-product-compliance
Lightning Source LLC
Chambersburg PA
CBHW020301170426
43202CB00008B/451